THE LITTLE BOOK OF
EPIC DAD JOKES

First published in 2025 by OH
An Imprint of HEADLINE PUBLISHING GROUP LIMITED

1

Disclaimer:

Cataloguing in Publication Data is available from the British Library

ISBN 978-1-03542-258-6

Compiled and written by: Malcolm Croft
Editorial: Saneaah Muhammad
Designed by: Tony Seddon
Project manager: Russell Porter
Production: Rachel Burgess
Printed and bound in Dubai

Headline's policy is to use papers that are natural, renewable and recyclable products and made from wood grown in well-managed forests and other controlled sources. The logging and manufacturing processes are expected to conform to the environmental regulations of the country of origin.

HEADLINE PUBLISHING GROUP LIMITED
An Hachette UK Company
Carmelite House, 50 Victoria Embankment, London EC4Y 0DZ

The authorised representative in the EEA is Hachette Ireland, 8 Castlecourt Centre, Dublin 15, D15 XTP3, Ireland (email: info@hbgi.ie)

www.headline.co.uk   www.hachette.co.uk

THE LITTLE BOOK OF
EPIC DAD
JOKES

SIMPLY THE BEST OF THE WORST

CONTENTS

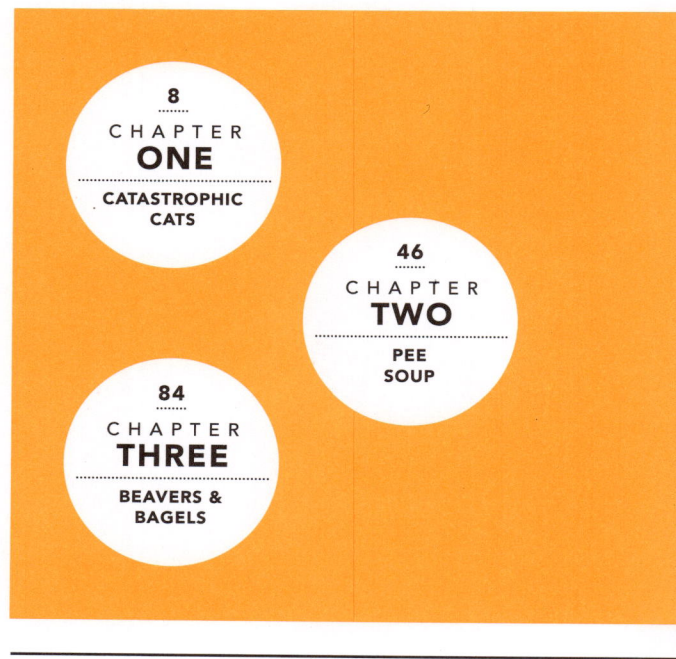

INTRODUCTION

Dear Dads,

What do you call shoes made of bananas?

Slippers

Dads have been torturing their terrified families with terribly silly jokes (like the one above) for decades, possibly even centuries, judging by the smell of some of the gags you'll find in many bog-standard joke books. They may have made your family guffaw or groan, with the odd titter or two. But, that's all. *YAWN!*

We think you deserve better! You deserve dad jokes that are huge, massive, GINORMOUS, the type of puns and larks that makes your ears cry with tears of joy. What you deserve is an EPIC dad joke book…

Hello!

Welcome to *The Little book of Epic Dad Jokes*… a tiny tome that is perfect for dad joke lovers looking to become connossieurs. The witty quips and cracks inside this book have been hand-picked by professionals and are the very, *very* best dad jokes you can buy over the counter without a prescription. Ignore the book's recommended retail price, we can assure you these dad jokes are priceless. And worth every penny.

So, grab a towel – you're going to need a large one – and a family member who needs cheering up (pick granddad, he's usually the grumpiest) and begin telling these epic bad boys one by one with wild, gluttonous abandon. Don't stop until the final page. We promise – nay, guarantee – that your family and friends will be leaking with glee as quickly as you can say squizzlefropulousmagnifitastiliciousquirkatronaut-sauerkrautwhimsyblenderbogglefluppinquibblebibble.

Yep, they're that EPIC. Enjoy!

CHAPTER
ONE

CATASTROPHIC CATS

Welcome to your first stop on this mega tour of epic dad jokery.

Now, don't worry, we'll ease you in gently. We don't want to knock your socks off too quickly – you may need them later to wipe your eyes, and possibly your bottom.

The dad jokes within this section have been graded LEVEL ONE on the Dad Joke Epicness Scale, so expect just a smidge of the absurd and a splash of the ridiculous. Nothing you can't handle, right? Giddy up!

What do you call a group of disorganized cats?

A cat-tastrophe.

WHAT DO YOU CALL A PILE OF CATS?

WHAT KIND OF TREE FITS IN YOUR HAND?

A palm tree!

What happens when you boil a funny bone?

What did the horse say after it tripped?

Help! I've fallen and I can't giddyup!

Why should you never use beef5tew as your computer password?

Did you know that Albert Einstein was a real person?

And you thought he was just a theoretical physicist!

What kind of dinosaur loves to sleep?

What do you call it when someone sneezes more than once?

A few.

What did the drummer name her twin daughters?

Why is there always a wall around cemeteries?

Because people are always dying to get in.

Why did the pickle wear sunglasses to the beach?

WHAT HAS HANDS BUT CAN'T CLAP?

A clock!

What do you get hanging off apple trees?

When do doctors get angry?

When they run out of patients.

HOW DO MEXICANS KEEP WARM?

Knock, knock.
Who's there?

Repeat.
Repeat, who?

Who, who,
who...

WHY IS THE OCEAN ALWAYS BLUE?

How do hens stay fit?

They always egg-cercise!

How do you kill a vegetarian vampire?

Why did the belt go to prison?

He held up a pair of trousers!

WHAT DID THE BEAVER SAY TO THE TREE?

WHAT KIND OF BAGEL CAN FLY?

A plain bagel.

What's the difference between roast beef and pea soup?

Anyone can roast beef,
but nobody can pee soup.

Why are snake races so exciting?

They're always neck and neck.

Knock, knock.

Who's there?

Nana.

Nana, who?

Nana your business.

Why was Jimmy fired from the banana factory?

He kept throwing away the bent ones.

Why should you never trust a pig with a secret?

Because it's bound to squeal.

Knock, knock.
Who's there?
Arya.
Arya, who?
Arya going to open the door?

Why are mummies scared of vacation?

They're afraid to unwind.

WHY DID THE ZOMBIE CROSS THE ROAD?

To get to the dead end.

Why are graveyards so noisy?

Because of all the coffin.

HOW DO TREES ACCESS THE INTERNET?

They log in.

WHAT KIND OF TEST DO ZOMBIES TAKE?

What's the leading cause of dry skin?

Towels.

What do you call a hen looking at a lettuce?

CHAPTER
TWO

PEE SOUP

You made it through chapter one! Phew! We thought you'd crash and burn.

But don't get too comfortable just yet. LEVEL TWO epicness now stands before you, ready to defeat and conquer your will to live.

Before you go any further, be warned, these dad jokes are so dangerously epic that they may cause mild flatulence in both you and your victim… but don't worry, it only lasts for a few days. Besides, it's the incontinence that you need to worry about. Let's go, before you start leaking…

What do you get when you cross a pig and a pineapple?

A porky pine!

WHAT DO YOU GET WHEN YOU COMBINE A PIG AND A COW?

Why did the chicken cross the playground?

To get to the other slide.

Knock, knock.
Who's there?
Woo.
Woo, who?
No need to cheer, it's just a joke!

WHAT IS BLACK AND WHITE AND BLACK AND WHITE AND BLACK AND WHITE AND BLACK AND WHITE?

A penguin, rolling down a hill.

Why was the broom late for work?

What is invisible and smells like carrots?

Rabbit farts.

What do you get when you put a sheep on a trampoline?

How are frying pans and Europe similar?

They both have Greece at the bottom.

Why don't fish play basketball?

Knock, knock.
Who's there?
Yodel ye.
Yodel ye, who?
I didn't know you could yodel!

Knock, knock.
Who's there?
Cows go.
Cows go who?
No, silly!
Cows go moo.

Why did the sentence fail its driving test?

It never came to a full stop.

What did the duck say after a meal?

HOW CAN YOU TELL IF A PIG IS HOT?

It's bacon.

Why are most people tired on April 1st?

They've just finished a 31-day March.

Knock, knock.
Who's there?
Ice cream soda.
Ice cream soda who?
Ice cream soda people can hear me!

WHAT FRUIT DO TWINS LOVE THE MOST?

Pears!

WHY DO TURKEYS HAVE GOOD RHYTHM?

They have drumsticks.

Why was the robot angry?

Because someone kept pressing his buttons!

What did the beach say when the tide came in?

Long time no sea.

What do you call two guys hanging out by your window?

WHY CAN'T CINDERELLA PLAY SOCCER?

Because she always runs away from the ball.

What do you call it when a cow grows facial hair?

What do you call a snail onboard a ship?

A snailor!

Why did the duck cross the road?

To prove that it was'nt a chicken.

What do you call 26 letters that went for a swim?

The alphawet.

WHEN WILL THE LITTLE SNAKE ARRIVE?

What do you call it when a group of apes starts a company?

WHAT DID THE PIG PUT ON HIS DRY SKIN?

What kind of noise does a witch's vehicle make?

Brrroooom, brrroooom.

Why does a Moon-rock taste better than an Earth-rock?

Because it's a little meteor.

WHY ARE GARDEN FENCES SAD?

They always get overlooked.

What creature is smarter than a talking parrot?

What always falls but is never clumsy?

The rain.

What do you call an elephant in a telephone booth?

CHAPTER
THREE

BEAVERS & BAGELS

Wait. Stop. You're at LEVEL THREE already? Wow! You must be a pro!

But don't get cocky kid, the dad jokes in this next chapter pack a serious crash-bang-wallop and enough firepower to make your funny bone go all floppy. We've seen it happen before.

To celebrate the halfway point of all this epicness, we recommend that you take a quick breather now. It may be the freshest air you breathe for some time... as this next set of jokes can get a little bit... stanky.

What do you call an eagle who can play the piano?

Talented!

It was a tie.

Why did no one win the neck-decorating contest?

Did you hear about the claustrophobic astronaut?

He needed a little space.

WHY CAN'T T-REX'S CLAP THEIR HANDS?

Because they're extinct.

What do you get when you cross a snowman and a shark?

Frostbite.

WHY DO DINOSAURS HIDE FROM SANTA'S REINDEER?

Because they're afraid of Comet.

WHY WAS IT CALLED "THE DARK AGES"?

Because of all the knights.

What do you call a nervous javelin thrower?

WHY WAS SANTA CRYING?

Because he stubbed his mistletoe.

WHAT DO YOU CALL A COW ON A TRAMPOLINE?

I didn't like my moustache at first.

But then it grew on me!

What did the doctor say to the gingerbread man who broke a leg?

What do you get when you cross a chicken with a skunk?

A fowl smell!

WHAT'S YELLOW AND LOOKS LIKE A PINEAPPLE?

A lemon with a new haircut.

What do you call bears with no ears?

B.

Why are humans so good at sleeping?

Why couldn't the lifeguard save the hippie?

He was too far out, man.

What do you get when you cross a bison with a chicken?

Knock, knock.
Who's there?
Cargo.
Cargo, who?
Cargo in the garage.

WHAT'S BLACK AND WHITE AND READ ALL OVER?

How do you get two whales in a car?

Start in England and drive west.

Why did the baker need to work so hard?

Because he kneaded to make some dough.

Why did the worker get fired from the orange juice factory?

Lack of concentration.

HOW DO MOUNTAINS SEE?

Why do hills never become mountains?

Because they peak to soon.

What goes tick-tick-woof-woof?

A watchdog.

WHAT DO YOU CALL A GREEDY PIG?

A hog.

Why don't bears wear hiking boots?

WHAT DO YOU CALL A GIRL STANDING BETWEEN TWO POSTS?

Annette.

What's red and bad for your teeth?

What do you call a musical group composed of dads?

A pop band!

WHAT DO YOU CALL A PIG WITH THREE EYES?

Piiig.

What's brown and sounds like a bell?

Dung!

Why did the house go to the doctor?

A sandwich walks into a bar. The bartender says "Sorry, we don't serve food here."

WHAT DO YOU GET WHEN TWO GIRAFFES COLLIDE?

CHAPTER
FOUR

KURT & ROD

Time to turn up the epicness.
Welcome to freakin' LEVEL FOUR!

It's all downhill from here, or uphill,
depending on what you think is worse or
if you're riding a bike.

Remember, take each joke one at
a time and if you need to take a break just
come back to this page, this safe space,
and stare at our lovely little drawing
of a banana – it always helps us calm to
down when we've over-indulged
in too much epicness.

Why are plants afraid of mathematics?

Because plants don't like square roots.

Why is the cheetah so bad at hide-and-seek?

Because it's always spotted.

Which is fastest: hot or cold?

Hot. You can catch a cold.

What instrument is found in the bathroom?

Why do cows wear bells?

Because their horns don't work.

What do you call your friend who stands in a hole?

What is a witch's most enjoyable subject in school?

Spelling!

WHAT DO YOU CALL A BEAR WITH NO TEETH?

A gummy bear!

What noise does a dizzy turkey make?

„Wobble, wobble."

Why doesn't Dracula have any friends?

Because he's a pain in the neck.

What kind of monkey can fly?

A hot air baboon!

How can you keep someone in suspense?

WHAT CAR DOES A SHEEP DRIVE?

A Lamborghini.

What has two words, starts with P, ends with E and has thousands of letters?

Knock, knock.
Who's there?

Mikey.
Mikey, who?

Mikey doesn't work. Can you let me in?

WHAT IS WORSE THAN FINDING A WORM IN YOUR APPLE?

What does a clock do when it's hungry?

It goes back four seconds!

WHAT DO YOU GET WHEN YOU CROSS AN ELEPHANT WITH A BEE?

What is the difference between a cat and a comma?

One has claws at the end of its paws, and the other is a pause at the end of a clause.

Knock, knock.
Who's there?
Car go.
Car go who?
Nah mate, Owl go who, Car go beep-beep

WHAT DO YOU CALL A PIG PLAYING TUG-OF-WAR?

Pulled pork.

WHAT DO YOU CALL A PENGUIN IN THE SAHARA DESERT?

Knock, knock
Who's there?

Figs.
Figs who?

Figs the doorbell, I've been knocking forever.

What do you get when you cross a river and a stream?

Which vegetable has the best kung-fu?

Broc-lee.

WHAT DO DENTISTS CALL THEIR X-RAYS?

Tooth pics!

How many dads does it take to screw in a light bulb?

Less than it takes to screw in a heavy one.

Did you hear about the man who was addicted to soap?

What do you call lettuce in space?

A saladellite.

WHAT HAPPENS WHEN DAD WAKES UP GRUMPY?

He apologizes for disturbing mum's lie in.

WHAT DO YOU CALL AN INDECISIVE BEE?

A maybee?

Why do seagulls fly over the sea?

If they flew over the bay, they would be bagels.

CHAPTER
FIVE

HOT AIR
BABOONS

WARNING! WARNING! DANGER! LEVEL
FIVE! THE POINT OF NO RETURN!

Congratulations guys and gals, you've
made it to the last set of jokes.
But you're on your own from here.
We can't follow you any further. It's been
nice knowing you, but only madness
lies ahead!

GOOD LUCK...and remember,
the banana will be with you...always!

Why did the melon jump into the lake?

It wanted to be a watermelon.

What's a scarecrow's favourite fruit?

Where do fish keep their cars on Sunday?

Carp Arks.

WHY DO THIEVES GET SO UPSET?

Can a frog jump higher than a house?

Of course, a house can't jump.

What do you call a sad strawberry?

Why does Batman never play poker?

In case the Joker shows up.

Why should you never cluck like a chicken?

Why should you never be late for lunch with cannibals?

They'll give you the cold shoulder.

What does an egg like to do for fun?

WHAT TYPE OF HOUSE WEIGHS THE LEAST?

A lighthouse.

What does Superman use to eat his soup?

What do you do when your bunny gets wet?

You get your hare dryer.

What does a house wear?

WHAT HAS A HEAD AND A TAIL, BUT NO BODY?

A coin.

Why did the pirates stop playing cards?

Because the captain was standing on the deck.

What do you call a bear that's stuck in the rain?

A drizzly bear.

Did you hear about the novel that felt unwell?

WHAT DID THE GREEN GRAPE SAY TO THE RED GRAPE?

"BREATH!"

What do you get if you stand between two llamas?

Why did the dinosaur cross the street?

Because the chicken was off sick.

WHAT DO YOU CALL A FAIRY WHO DOESN'T LIKE BATHS?

Why can't you hear a pterodactyl using the bathroom?

Because the P is silent.

What's the difference between a piano and a fish?

You can tune a piano but you can't tuna fish.

Why did the dog bark at the sandpaper?

Because it was ruff!

How was the snow globe feeling after the storm?

HOW DOES A TRAIN EAT ITS FOOD?

Chew-chew!

What is fast, loud and crunchy?

WHAT DO YOU CALL AN ANT WHO FIGHTS CRIME?

A vigilanty!

What do you call a man with a shovel?

My dog is a genius. I asked him, "What's two minus two?" He said nothing.

Why did the ice-cream truck break down?

WHY IS COLLECTING LEAVES A GOOD JOB?

You can rake it in.

Why did the man run around his bed?

Because he was trying to catch up on his sleep!

How do you make a hot-dog stand?

Take away its chair.